You Can Become
a
Dynamic Intercessor

Workbook for *Rees Howells, Intercessor* (1993 edition)

You Can Become a D~~y~~nam~~i~~c Intercessor

Workbook for *Rees Howells, Intercessor* (1993 edition)

by

Mina Kohlhafer

CHRISTIAN ❖ LITERATURE ❖ CRUSADE
Fort Washington, Pennsylvania 19034

CHRISTIAN LITERATURE CRUSADE

U.S.A.
P.O. Box 1449, Fort Washington, PA 19034

GREAT BRITAIN
51 The Dean, Alresford, Hants., SO24 9BJ

AUSTRALIA
P.O. Box 91, Pennant Hills, N.S.W. 2120

NEW ZEALAND
10 MacArthur Street, Feilding

ISBN 0-87508-299-8

Copyright © 1989
Mina Kohlhafer

This Printing 1997

PRINTED IN THE UNITED STATES OF AMERICA

Contents

YOU CAN BECOME A DYNAMIC INTERCESSOR!

Workbook to *Rees Howells, Intercessor* (1993 Edition)

For Use Individually or in a Group

How to Use This Workbook:

General: Locating of paragraphs and
Reading aloud from the book.

1. Paragraph count is always from the first full paragraph on the page; leftovers from the previous page are not counted.
2. When reading paragraphs aloud, always continue on to the next page from the bottom paragraph when necessary.

Studying as an Individual

1. You don't have to be a Bible scholar to understand and be blessed by the Word of God or a spiritual biography like this; you just have to be willing to allow the Holy Spirit to be your teacher.
2. Set up a daily time schedule for prayer and fellowship with God, followed by your study of one or more chapters.
3. Use the workbook as your reading guide.
4. Look up all the Bible verses as you come to them and meditate on each one.
5. As you read each chapter, focus your attention on the paragraphs to be read aloud.
6. Write out answers to the questions that follow.
7. When there is a Discussion or Personal question, give the answer out loud so you can be blessed as you hear the answer.

8. Do each assignment as it comes up, so that the Lord will be able to point out the areas in your life that need to be changed.

Studying as a Group

1. Why should I read the designated chapters beforehand?
   So I can have an overall view of the chapter and be ready to participate.
2. Why do we need to read the specified paragraphs out loud in class?
   As we hear the truth of God's Word or of His dealings with Rees Howells, it is able to penetrate our hearts and bring us to that blessed position where great and mighty revelations can enter in.
3. Should I fill in the blanks at home or in class?
   Do it in class, as each specific area is discussed.
4. How do I benefit from doing the assignments at the end of each chapter at home by myself?
   You will allow the Holy Spirit to speak to you during the week and bring those things to your attention that need changing.

As a Quick Review Manual

1. When in need of a spiritual uplift, or a quick assist in getting back into the power place of God, thumb through the workbook and read only those items in the boxed areas.

SUGGESTED READING/STUDY GUIDE FOR SIXTEEN WEEKS

Week #	Chapters
1.	Foreword, Ch. 1, 2
2.	Ch. 3, 4
3.	Ch. 5, 6
4.	Ch. 7, 8, 9
5.	Ch. 10, 11, 12
6.	Ch. 13, 14, 15
7.	Ch. 16, 17, 18
8.	Ch. 19, 20
9.	Ch. 21, 22
10.	Ch. 23, 24
11.	Ch. 25, 26
12.	Ch. 27, 28, 29
13.	Ch. 30, 31, 32
14.	Ch. 33, 34
15.	Ch. 35, 36
16.	Ch. 37, Conclusion

Helpful Suggestions for the Leader

You don't have to be a Bible scholar or a trained Bible teacher for God to use you mightily as a Bible study leader. You just have to be willing, and to acknowledge the Holy Spirit as the teacher.

Zechariah 4:6c "Not by might, nor
by power, but by my Spirit, says the
Lord Almighty."

1. Start on time, and allow approximately two hours per session.
2. Suggested class size would be six to eighteen people, in an atmosphere of peace and quiet, without interruptions. Have the people sit in a circle—around a table, or in a living room, family room, or small cozy church room.
3. This workbook is based on the New International Version of the Bible, but we suggest using many versions as you read, and that you identify them before reading.
4. Also have a dictionary on hand to look up words you don't know.
5. Everyone should have a book and a workbook of his own.
6. Having a pitcher of ice water and paper cups available is a nice touch.
7. Start with prayer, and as you get to know the members of the group you might call on various ones of them to pray.
8. If desired, allow a time at the beginning for one or two very short testimonies of what happened during the week to point out a truth from the lesson.
9. As leader, you read the informative and instructive parts of the workbook aloud in class and see that everyone takes a turn reading the Bible verses, paragraphs from the book, and answering the questions.
10. Direct the Discussion and Personal Questions to the whole group. To get more response you might ask a specific person: "What do you think?" or "How would you do it?" Encourage all members to participate, but do not push.
11. Especially emphasize the items in the workbook that are enclosed in a box.
12. If someone starts talking about personal problems, and gets off the subject, be loving but firm in getting them back into the lesson. Time is very precious.

13. Don't be afraid of controversy, but also don't spend a lot of time trying to find an impossible answer. If you don't know the answer, say so, and state that you will check it out and try to have the answer for the next session; and do so.

14. Never say an opinion is wrong. Say you don't agree and ask what scripture the person bases his viewpoint on, and if possible give a scripture to prove your point of view.

15. As you finish each chapter, read the assignments out loud to the class. Do not give out an assignment unless the chapter has been completed.

16. At the end of each class, specify which chapters are to be read at home next and remind them which assignments are to be done (see suggested chapter reading guide).

17. Go over the assignments at the start of the next session, prior to beginning a new study. Call on only one or two students for their assignment answers, and give yours last as a summary.

INTRODUCTION

When the Lord first spoke to me to teach a Bible study on prayer, and use the book *Rees Howells, Intercessor* as my guide, I was not an intercessor. I didn't even know what the word "intercessor" meant.

I never expected to be an intercessor, as I thought to be one you had to be somebody special.

Moses, Joshua, Daniel, Jesus, and Paul were all intercessors (Exodus 32:9-14, Joshua 7:6-10, Daniel 9:1-23, John 17:1-26, Colossians 1:9-12). Yes, they were special, but *all* of God's children are special. All that was available to them is also available to you.

> **Isaiah 50:4-5** "The Sovereign Lord has given me an instructed tongue, to know the word that sustains the weary. He wakens me morning by morning, wakens my ear to listen like one being taught. The Sovereign Lord has opened my ears, and I have not been rebellious; I have not drawn back."

God loves you and wants you to walk in health and happiness. As you faithfully come into His presence daily for worship, fellowship, and guidance, a miraculous change will occur in your heart and mind. The energy of eternity and the resurrection power of Jesus will come, making you in thought and deed and prayer-power more like Jesus.

Now, you are the one being taught! You are the one whose ears are being opened! You are the one who is obedient, I trust, and you are the one who is going to reach the throne of God for those in need!

I am becoming the intercessor God is seeking . . . and so shall you.

Mina Kohlhafer

Read the FOREWORD

Prayer:
"Heavenly Father, in the name of Your Son Jesus . . . pour Your light into our souls, and don't let us waver regarding Your promises, but strengthen our faith. Let us be transformed into His likeness more and more each day, and let Your glory shine through. Thank You, Lord."

This verse sums up Rees Howells' life:
Romans 4:20 "Yet he did not waver through unbelief regarding the promise of God, but was strengthened in his faith and gave glory to God."

This verse can pertain to each one of us:
2 Corinthians 3:18 "And we, who with unveiled face all reflect the Lord's glory, are being transformed into his likeness with ever-increasing glory, which comes from the Lord, who is the Spirit."

The Foreword describes Rees Howells as being "beyond measure large-hearted."

Read 1 Kings 3:5-14, Psalm 119:32 (KJV & NIV).
1.   Who enlarges our hearts and sets them free? _____
Discussion Question: Why do I need a spiritually enlarged heart?

Page 9, paragraph 3: "I remember one young Christian asking him how he knew God's voice, and he said, 'Can't you tell your mother's voice from any other?' 'Yes, of course,' the young man answered. 'Well, I know His voice just like that.' "

> **Hearing the voice of God is foremost in walking in the operation of the gifts of the Spirit, but more especially in intercessory prayer made under the Spirit's guidance.**

1

2

You should be able to discern God's voice from all others. God spoke to
Adam, Noah, Abraham, Moses, Joshua, Samuel, Elijah, Isaiah,
Ezekiel, Peter, James, John, Paul, and many others.

Read Exodus 33:9, Numbers 7:89.
Read John 10:4-5, 27-28.

Personal Question: Are you one of these sheep?
Personal Question: Can you also expect to hear God's voice?

You can hear and be guided by God's voice.

Read Psalm 46:10.
2.   What do I have to do to know God? _____

Read Proverbs 8:34.
3.   What do I get for listening to God? _____

4.   Complete: I am told to _____ and to _____

Read Psalm 32:8.
5.   List four things God said He would do for you:

      a. _____ b. _____ c. _____ d. _____

Read Isaiah 58:11.
6.   Rewrite this verse, inserting your name in appropriate places:

      _____
      _____
      _____
      _____

7.   List some of the qualities of water, especially spring water:

      _____
      _____

Discussion Question: What does it mean *for you* to be like a well-watered
garden, like a spring whose waters never fail?

This is the kind of relationship that is available to you when you
listen to God—taking time to be still and quiet, and making
yourself available to hear what He has to say, and most
important, being obedient.

Read Chapter 1: EARLY YEARS

Page 11. Rees Howells was born in 1879, in South Wales.
> Wales is the smallest of Great Britain's three countries. It is bounded on the east by England, and is made up of coastal plains, deep lush valleys, coal-mining and industrial areas . . . beautiful, harsh mountains and lonely uplands. Its main cities are Cardiff and Swansea.

Page 11, last paragraph, first sentence: read aloud.
1.   What two things were preeminent in the Howells' family life?

_____

Discussion Question: What would happen in our nation if this were true in the majority of homes?
2.   List some of the dramatic changes that would take place:

_____

_____

Personal Question: How would it affect your home?

Page 14, paragraph 2, read aloud.
Discussion Question: How do you stay "under the influence of God"?

Page 15, last sentence:
> "But is it not God who turns the *ordinary* into the *extraordinary* when He is given a chance?"

Read 1 Corinthians 2:9-10.
Discussion Question: What do these verses mean to you?
Personal Question: What can you foresee God bringing forth in you?
> **Assignment:**
> Write a prayer for your nation on "Godliness and love in the home."

_____

_____

4

_____

_____

_____

_____

_____

(Try to use this in your daily prayers.)

Read Chapter 2: TWO SHOCKS

Page 18, last paragraph, read aloud.
"And until there is a conviction of need, there can never be a desire for a change. But God has *His* ways!"
Consider this last sentence in relation to all the people you want to see saved. Pray and believe.

> **Know that God has His ways of dealing with each individual.**

Discussion Question: What are some of the ways God has worked in your life to bring about a conviction of need?

Page 20, paragraph 3, read aloud.
1.   What frequency and quality of correspondence do you have with God?

Personal Question: What can you do today to improve this correspondence?

If you are not born again . . .
ask Jesus to forgive your sins and
take control of your life right now . . .
and correspondence will begin!

Read Psalm 25:5, John 16:13, 1 Corinthians 2:7,10 (LB).
Discussion Question: What is available to you from God?
Assignment:
Write a prayer for an individual who is in need of knowing God, but doesn't have a desire to change.

_____

_____

_____

_____

Now . . . write a prayer for yourself, for God to show you how to deal with this person.

_____

_____

_____

_____

_____

_____

_____

Read Chapter 3: MEETING THE RISEN LORD

Page 22, paragraph 1, read aloud.

> **Only a personal Savior
> can take you
> to the other side.**

Page 24, paragraphs 2 and 3, regarding *praying* or *complaining*, read aloud.

1. Which will avail you more? _____ Why? _____
    _____

    Remember this the next time you are in a bad situation: Pray for the
    people enmeshed in it, rather than complain, and the Holy Spirit will
    change the circumstances!

2. In the story of Maurice Reuben, circle the two things that stand out in
    his relationship to God:

    uneasiness   total obedience   kindness   hearing God's voice

Page 26, paragraphs 1 through 4, read aloud.

> **Can you say with Rees Howells:
> "The Savior became everything to me"?**

Read 2 Corinthians 5:17-20, 1 John 2:2.

3. List the qualities of a truly born-again person: _____
    _____
    _____

4. Look up the word *reconcile:* _____
    _____

7

8

Page 26, paragraph 4, says: "I changed altogether . . . the veil was taken back, my eyes were opened, and I *saw* Him."

Read the following verses and you will also see and hear Jesus:
Luke 1:30-33, 2:10-11, 2:40, 3:21-22, 4:1, 4:17-21.

> **Jesus' offices of prophet, priest and king
> originated on earth,
> but continue in heaven.**

Jesus is our Prophet as He communicates God's will and discloses the future to God's children.
Read Deuteronomy 18:15-20, Matthew 13:57.

Jesus is our Great High Priest and Intercessor and draws near to the Father to plead on behalf of men.
Read Hebrews 4:14-16, 7:22-25, John 17:7-9; discuss John.

Jesus is our soon-coming King.
Read Revelation 17:14, Zechariah 14:9.

Page 27, paragraphs 1 and 2, read aloud. Notice especially:
"He would love sinners through me, as He loved me."
Personal Question: Is Jesus loving sinners through you?

Page 27, last paragraph, read aloud.
Discussion Question: What has claims on your time?

> **Time well spent—
> being mindful of the needs of others,
> always handling the situation as Jesus would—
> this is putting God first.**

Assignment:
Check below those things which would *not* be a priority to God for your time:
( ) Watching soap operas
( ) Pulling weeds and praying in the Spirit
( ) Taking a thorn out of a child's foot

( ) Reading the Bible
( ) Spending unprofitable time on the phone
( ) Grumbling as you do the wash
( ) Praising as you do the wash
( ) Keeping bitterness in your mind for hours
( ) Cooking or eating fancy food that adds weight
( ) Praying for the nation as you clean or cut the lawn
( ) Washing dishes and praying
( ) Taking out the rubbish and praying for neighbor
( ) Reading novels that do not glorify God
( ) Meditating on the Word

In all instances, be led by the Holy Spirit, and be a doer of the Word!

Read Chapter 4: THE WELSH REVIVAL

Page 29, paragraphs 2 and 3, read aloud.
1.   What are the two hindrances to blessing?

     a. _____ b. _____

Read John 14:23, Luke 6:37.
Personal Question: What are the main hindrances in your life that keep
God's blessings from overtaking you?

> Obedience to the promptings of the Spirit and
> open confession of Christ brought down the blessing.

> Jesus forgives instantly . . . so should we!!!

Read Psalm 119:165 (KJV).
Nothing should offend us when we are walking in the love of God. Don't let
    the devil get your mind and cause you to use up God's valuable time by
    dwelling on vain imaginations, resentments or other bitterness.

> **Don't dwell on any unlovely thoughts.**

Page 30, paragraphs 1 and 2, read aloud.
Read Acts 2:1, 8:5-8 (both in KJV).
2.   What is to be the main aim in all we are doing? _____
Page 31, first paragraph, read aloud.

> **The intercession of the Holy Ghost**
> **for the saints in this present evil**
> **world must be made through believers**
> **filled with the Holy Ghost.**

Page 31, last sentence: Rees said, ". . . we felt the lack of power for service."

Discussion Question: What do you think he meant by this?

Read Acts 1:8.
3. Where does the power come from? _____

Read Acts 1:5, 5:32.
4. Complete: God gives His Holy Spirit to those who _____ Him.

> **Assignment:**
> Look at someone who is filled mightily with the Holy Spirit, and list what God does through him as a yielded,
>
> obedient vessel: _____
>
> _____
>
> _____
>
> _____
>
> **Personal Question:** Would you like God to work through you in this way?
> What two things that we discussed above will you have
>
> to walk in? a. _____ b. _____

Read Chapter 5: THE HOLY GHOST TAKES POSSESSION

Page 33, paragraph 3: "Rees was in a meeting . . . where a young woman read Romans 8:26-30."
Read Romans 8:26-30.
"As Rees listened, he said to himself, 'I know I am predestined according to the foreknowledge of God, and justified—but am I glorified?' "

Read John 12:23-28.
1. Look up the word "glorified" in a Bible Dictionary and discuss what it means.

Personal Question: Consider what you do in your personal life that does not glorify God. What can you do to change it?

Read 1 Corinthians 10:31, John 17:21-23.

> To be glorified now is to be rid of self and continually partaking of the Divine nature . . . in constant communion with the Father so that the manifestation of God's power is flowing through one at all times.

Page 34, paragraphs 1 and 2, read aloud.

Discussion Question: Do you see a present aspect of glorification, as Rees did?

> There is a place for you.

Read Ephesians 2:1-6.

Page 34, paragraphs 3 and 4, read aloud.

Read 1 Corinthians 6:19, Romans 12:1.

Page 35, paragraph 2, read aloud.
2.   What two things does the Holy Spirit bring in when you allow him to?

a. _____ b. _____

Discussion Question: What wondrous things could be wrought in our families, cities and nation if these two powers were at work within us?

> **It has to be an unconditional surrender.**
> **Only the Holy Ghost in me can live like the Savior.**

Page 36, paragraph 3, read aloud.
Prayer for cleansing: In the Name of Jesus, we ask that You cleanse our hearts and open our minds to the light of Your Word. Deliver us from self and fill us with Your Holy Spirit. . . .

> **The Holy Spirit exposed the root of my nature, which is "self." Sin was already canceled, so it wasn't sin He was dealing with; it was "self."**

3. What is sin? _____

4. What is self? _____
Personal Question: How can self be exposed and gotten rid of?
For the results of turning your life over to the Holy Spirit, read 2 Peter 1:4 in the Living Bible and the NIV.

> **Then came the process of sanctification . . .**
> **Step by step, the self nature was replaced with God's Divine nature.**

5.   Look up the word "sanctify": _____
Look up Psalm 51:10 (KJV), and write it here to use as a daily prayer.

_____

_____

Page 38, paragraph 1, read aloud.

14

6.　Look up the word "temporal": _____

_____

7.　On page 38, paragraph 2, what must go for the Holy Spirit to come in?

_____

Personal Question: Can you say with Rees: "Lord, I am willing"?

Page 39, paragraph 3, read aloud.
8.　List what dynamic things happened when the Third Person of the Godhead came in:

　　a.　_____

　　b.　_____

　　c.　_____

　　d.　_____

Page 39, paragraph 5, read aloud.
9.　How can you better exalt the Savior in your daily life? _____

_____

_____

Page 39, paragraph 6, read aloud.
Discussion Question: How has God's love worked in your life, and how can it work in the lives of those you are praying for?

> That same Holy Ghost who had entered the apostles on the day of Pentecost had entered him, and would produce similar results!

Personal Question: Can God do this for you?

Streams of living waters flow out of those in whom the Spirit dwells — read John 7:37-39.

We have been talking about being *sanctified,* or meeting the qualifications for the *royal priesthood.*
Read 1 Peter 2:9, Deuteronomy 7:6.

Assignment:
List the duties of the Old Testament priests:

_____

_____

_____

List the duties that compare, as you function in the office of a Holy Spirit-filled priest:

_____

_____

_____

_____

Read Chapter 6: LOVING AN OUTCAST

Page 41, first paragraph, read aloud.
1. What two objectives has the new owner?

   a. _____ b. _____

2. Look up the word "cultivate": _____

3. Look up the word "fruitful": _____

Discussion Question: Compare these definitions to what God has been doing in your life.

> We are like a potentially beautiful garden, but can only produce fruit after being carefully cultivated so that the weeds are all removed.

4. List some of the things you might call weeds in your life: _____

   _____

   _____

> **The meaning of prayer is "answer."**

Effectual prayer must be guided praying.

Page 41, paragraph 3: "He was never again to ask God to answer a prayer through others if He could answer it through him."

Discussion Question: How could this apply to everyday circumstances?

Page 42, first paragraph, read aloud.

> **Love not by word or in tongue, but by deed and in truth.**

When the Holy Ghost comes in, He brings in the love of the Savior.

Read John 3:16, 15:13, 1 Corinthians 13:4-7, Colossians 3:12-14.

Page 42, paragraph 5, read aloud.
5.   What would the Lord have you do in your household in order to let
Him know you trust Him? _____

_____

> If you love one, you can love many; and if many,
> you can love all.

Page 43, paragraph 2, states: "The second outstanding prayer the Holy
Ghost prayed through him was for a man who went by the name of Jim
Stakes. . . . The Holy Spirit gave Rees Howells his first lesson in
'princely giving.'"
Read aloud this and the next two paragraphs (page 44).

> **It was a conflict
> between God and the devil
> for a soul.**

Personal Question: Can you look at each person, whether bad or good, and
see him as a precious soul?

Page 44, paragraphs 3-5, and page 45, paragraphs 1 and 2, read aloud.
Discussion Question: When has the "joy of heaven" come down on you for
obeying the Holy Spirit?

Page 45, paragraph 4, mentions: Love had conquered!
Situations aren't changed by criticisms or sharp words . . .
only by the Love of Jesus radiating from you.
Personal Question: Do you walk in this kind of love?

Prayer: Lord Jesus, help me to walk in your love and to show it forth to all I
meet, especially those in my family.

Page 45, paragraph 5, says: "Some of the worst characters gave their hearts
to the Lord."

Page 46, last paragraph, read aloud.
6.   List the three items of guided praying:

a. _____

b. _____

c. _____

18

Assignment:
Pray for the people listed below with these three things in
mind . . . and expect an answer!

As the Lord brings people to mind that need prayer for salvation, list them.

Date	Name	Date & Type of Answer

Read Chapter 7: A VILLAGE UNTOUCHED BY THE REVIVAL

Page 49, first paragraph, read aloud.
Discussion Question: What does it mean to be a good shepherd?

> **The Holy Ghost was going there, and He had authority to cast out devils and forgive sins.**

1. How does the Holy Spirit get into a situation? _____

_____

Read John 14:12, Mark 16:17-18.

Page 50, paragraphs 1 and 2, read aloud.
2. Complete: These young people were coming with _____

_____ .

Discussion Question: How can we "live out the Bible" to people?

Page 50, paragraph 6, through paragraph 1 of page 51, read aloud.

3. Complete: When he saw the _____ , he was touched

on a vital spot and _____ .

4. What breaks bondages? _____

   "He shall receive an hundredfold now in this time."

5. Do you believe this can still happen? _____

Page 52, paragraphs 1 and 2, read aloud.

> **Cut the ropes and take the promises. The Holy Ghost showed me that if God wanted me to go anywhere, He would surely provide the means.**

We can never really be "bondservants" until God does control our means.

Page 52, paragraphs 3 and 4, read aloud.

6.   Complete: His extremity was God's _____

7.   He now had a claim on God's resources _____

> **What joy I had in finding that
> I had finished with the limited resources
> of man and begun on the
> unlimited resources of God!**

Assignment:
Find two promises in the Bible that are better than "money in the bank."

1. _____

_____

_____

2. _____

_____

_____

Read Chapter 8: THE TRAMPS

Pages 55 and 56, Summary:

Rees was used to four good meals a day and God called him to a day of prayer and fasting.

When midday came he was on his knees in his bedroom, but there was no prayer that next hour. "I didn't know such a lust was in me. My agitation was the proof of the grip it had on me."

Rees disobeyed the Holy Spirit and went to lunch. He came face to face with disobedience to the Holy Ghost. To some people there might seem nothing in it, but once you are God's channel, on no account can you disobey Him or bring in your own ideas.

Discussion Question: Why should we not get ahead of God or use our own ideas?

Page 56, paragraph 2, read aloud.

Discussion Question: Tell what stands out in this paragraph, so far as you are concerned.

Personal Question: How can you apply it to your own life?

Page 56, paragraphs 3 and 4, read aloud.

> **To love the unlovely ones.**

Read 1 John 4:7-21, and in your Bible circle all the times the word "love" is mentioned.

1. What is the main thought of these verses? _____

_____

2. Why is God so strong in His command that we "love all people"?

_____

> **The identification of the intercessor
> with the ones for whom he prays
> requires feeling as they feel . . . sitting where they sit.**

21

Page 58, paragraphs 3 and 4, speak about "resting faith." Read aloud, starting with "The illustration. . . ."

Write a summary of how you personally have come through each of these positions, and where you are now.

Struggling _____

_____

Clinging _____

_____

Resting _____

_____

Read Hebrews 4:9-11, Isaiah 30:15.
Page 59, paragraphs 2 and 3, read aloud.
Page 60, paragraph 3, read aloud.

Disappointments are part of our training.

Assignment:
List some of the disappointments of your life that turned into valuable lessons.

_____

_____

_____

_____

_____

_____

_____

_____

_____

_____

_____

_____

Read Chapter 9: BINDING THE STRONG MAN

Page 63, first paragraph, read aloud.
1.   What did the Spirit tell Rees to do for the woman? _____

_____

Page 63, paragraph 2, read aloud.
2.   Complete: The Lord told him he was to use _____

_____ , but to reach her by _____ .

Read Matthew 12:29, John 15:7 (in KJV and NIV).

3.   Look up the word "abiding": _____

_____

Page 63, paragraph 3, through paragraph 1 of page 64, read aloud.

```
The promise is unlimited,
but its fulfillment depends on the abiding.
```

Read 1 John 2:6.
Write what it means in your own words: _____

_____

_____

Page 64, paragraphs 2 and 3, read aloud.
4.   How did Mr. Howells maintain this abiding? _____

_____

5.   What would the Holy Spirit then do? _____

_____

_____

Read John 15:10, 1 Peter 1:22.

Read John 15:5-8.

6.   Where does the power come from? _____

7.   What can you do without Jesus? _____

8.   What has to remain in us to get our wishes? _____

9.   What gives glory to God? _____

> **As an intercessor remains united to Jesus by abiding in Him, His power operates through the intercessor and accomplishes what needs to be done.**

Page 65, first paragraph, read aloud.
10.   Who was engaging the enemy in battle?

Page 65, paragraphs 3 and 4, read aloud.
Discussion question: What does "daily dying" mean?

Read Ephesians 6:12.
11.   Who is your adversary? _____

_____

_____

Read John 12:31-32.
12.   Who is going to be driven out of this world? _____

_____

Read Romans 16:20.

13.   Whom will God crush under our feet? _____

Read Revelation 20:10.
14.   What is the devil's doom? _____

Page 65, paragraph 6, read aloud.
Read 2 Chronicles 32:7-8.
15.   Who is your great unseen power? _____

Discussion Question: Could you pray for a desperate situation, totally by way of God's throne, and not in any way by hand or mouth try to influence it?

Page 65, last paragraph, read aloud.

16. Complete:
    a. It was now a case of _____ before the victory.
    b. The Holy Spirit did not allow him to pray; it would have been a
       _____ of _____ .
Discussion Question: What does it mean to "pray a prayer of doubt"?

Page 66, paragraphs 1 and 2, read aloud.
17. Look up Zechariah 4:6 and write the key portion here:

_____
_____
_____

Memorize this and know it is always by God's Spirit that things of God are
brought forth!

Page 67, paragraphs 2 and 3, read aloud.
Page 67, paragraphs 4 and 5, read aloud.
Discussion Question: Tell some of the things that have happened to you
    when you were obedient to the Spirit's leading.

**The Lord did more in a few minutes
through their obedience
than might have been done in hours without it.**

Assignment:
Look up the word "obedience" in a Bible Concordance,
and see how many times it is used. Then pick out two of
the most dynamic verses that show the power of
obedience and write them out below:

1. _____
   _____
   _____
   _____

2. _____
   _____
   _____
   _____

Read Chapter 10: A BRANCH IN THE VINE

Page 69, first paragraph, read aloud.
Discussion Question: How do you grieve the Spirit?

You are a branch in the Savior.
The branch gets nothing—
it is the needy that get the fruit.
Whatever the Father wants to
pour out to the world through you, He can do.

Personal Question: Are you coming into that position where God can flow
through you into the needy?

Page 71, paragraph 2, says: "His needs were to be made known only by way
of the Throne."
Discussion Question: How would that command affect your life?

Page 71, paragraph 3, through paragraph 1 of page 72, read aloud.

1.   Complete: There is no closer relationship than between a _____

      and a _____ .

2.   _____ am the branch and _____ is the vine.
3. Who gets the fruit you produce?

Read 2 Corinthians 5:17 in LB and NIV.
Discussion Question: How is God accomplishing this in your life?

> **Assignment:**
> In the block below, illustrate your relationship to Jesus.
> Draw a vine and label it Jesus. Make it thick and full of
> sap, which is the power of the Holy Spirit. Draw a branch
> coming out to one side, which is you, receiving the sap.

Draw a fruit on the end of your branch, which came from the power in the vine; and below, reaching up, draw a needy person.

When you look at this, remember, the only way the needy can get fruit from Jesus is when you are a functioning branch, flowing with power from the energy source!

Read Chapter 11: THE TUBERCULAR WOMAN

Page 73, first paragraph, read aloud.
Page 73, paragraph two, says, "Up to that time the Holy Spirit had never
  given him any prayers for healing."
1.   What kind of prayers had he been praying up to this time?

_____

Page 73, last paragraph, read aloud.
2.   Complete: a. He was daily in prayer for how long? _____
     This necessitated:
                b. A daily _____

                c. A daily _____

                d. A daily _____
Discussion Question: What does it mean to "go through"?

Read Matthew 8:16-17.
     Why should there not be freedom from the power and dominion of
     sickness?

> **The Holy Spirit can only make
> intercession through those human temples
> He indwells.**

     As an intercessor, a person must enter into the sufferings and take the
     place of the one prayed for.
Discussion Question: Have you ever been in this position? How have you
     handled it?

Page 77, paragraphs 4 and 5, read aloud.
3.   "The room was filled with His glory." What were the circumstances
     that allowed the glory of God to fill that room?

Page 78, paragraphs 2 and 3, read aloud.
Page 79, paragraph 2, last sentence, read aloud.

Discussion Question: How can a funeral be the beginning of resurrection life?

Page 79, last paragraph, read aloud.

> **Assignment:**
> Write out what this means to you: "The first case of healing, the first-fruits of this intercession, belonged to the Lord and had to go to the altar." _____
>
> _____
>
> _____
>
> _____
>
> _____
>
> _____
>
> _____
>
> _____

Read Chapter 12: WHAT IS AN INTERCESSOR?

Page 81, first paragraph, read aloud.
1. What was the central truth which the Holy Ghost gradually revealed

    to Mr. Howells? _____
2. What two things did the Spirit constantly lead him into?

    a. _____

    b. _____

God seeks intercessors . . . but seldom finds them.

Read Isaiah 59:16, Ezekiel 22:30.
Page 81, last paragraph, read aloud.
3. What are the three things to be seen in an intercessor which are not
    necessarily found in ordinary prayer?

    a. _____

    b. _____

    c. _____

Pages 82 and 83, summary:
Jesus is our Divine Intercessor
interceding for a lost world.

Read Hebrews 7:25.
God provided our Intercessor. Now He expects us to intercede for
others who are unable to *identify* with Jesus, or are not interested in the
agony, or are unequipped with the *authority.*

Identification is the first law of the
intercessor. He pleads effectively because he gives his life for those he
pleads for; he is their genuine representative; he has submerged his self-

> interest in their needs and sufferings, and as far as possible has literally *taken their place.*

> *Agony* is to be found present only in the Holy Spirit, as Intercessor on earth, and He can work only through those whose hearts are His dwelling place.

"Self" has to go to the cross, to be released from itself, in order to become the agent of the Holy Ghost. It is no theoretical death but a real crucifixion with Christ, with a "new man" coming to live on this earth!

Read Galatians 2:20.
Page 83, first full paragraph, read aloud.

4. Write below the most dynamic pair of sentences of this paragraph:

_____

_____

_____

_____

_____

_____

_____

_____

5. List some of the concerns for others you know you should have, but don't yet have: _____

_____

_____

_____

6. What is the root of this unconcern? _____

Discussion Question: How can this be overcome?

32

Page 84, paragraph 1, says:
> Intercession is more than the Spirit sharing His groanings with us and living His life of sacrifice for the world through us. *It is the Spirit gaining His ends of abundant grace.*

7.   Look up the word *grace* : _____

_____

Page 84, paragraph 1, also talks about *authority.*
Read John 12:21-26.
Discussion Question: How can this "law of the kernel of wheat and harvest" give you authority?

Page 84, paragraph 2, says:
> "There has only ever been one substitute for a world of sinners, Jesus the Son of God. But intercession so identifies the intercessor with the sufferer that it gives him a prevailing place with God. *He moves God.*"

8.   Look up the word *prevailing* : _____

_____

Page 84, paragraph 2, starting with "Thus Moses," read aloud.

9.   What is the most dynamic portion of this paragraph? _____

_____

_____

Page 84, the last paragraph, talks about "the gained position of intercession."
10. List below the four steps:

a. _____

b. _____

c. _____

d. _____

**The weak channel
is clothed with authority by the
Holy Ghost and can speak the word of
deliverance.**

Read John 14:12.
Jesus fulfills all of the four steps detailed above:

> The price is paid.
> Read Luke 23:44-46.
>
> The obedience is fulfilled.
> Read Matthew 26:42.

The inner wrestlings and groanings take their full course.
Read Mark 14:32-34.

> Then "the word of the Lord comes."
> Read John 19:30.

Page 85, paragraph 1, read aloud.
11. Contrast the two:
    a. The grace of faith: _____

    _____

    _____

    b. The gifts of faith: _____

    _____

    _____

Page 85, paragraph 2, the last sentence says (regarding George Muller and his intercession for the needs of the orphans): "The doors of God's Treasury had been permanently opened to him, and he could take as much as he needed."
Discussion Question: What kind of preparation would God have to do in your life before you could handle this type of relationship?

Page 85, last paragraph to end of chapter, read aloud.
Discussion Question: What were the various areas he had to gain before the final victory of access to the Throne?
Personal Question: Can you apply this principle to your circumstances at home or on the job?

Assignment:
To keep on keeping on and stay in God's presence when circumstances seem against you, what would you do in

the following cases? Choose one of the following: pray, praise, gripe, thank.

1. Harsh words are spoken   _____

2. Complimentary words spoken   _____

3. Car gets dent in fender   _____

4. Dinner burns   _____

5. Money is spent unwisely   _____

6. Unexpected company arrive   _____

7. You inherit $6,000   _____

Read Chapter 13: CHALLENGING DEATH

Page 87, paragraph 2, read aloud.
Discussion Question: Why do you have to weep?

Page 87, fourth paragraph, over to page 88, up to "The wife came down
... "—read aloud.
Discussion Question: Describe what God's presence has felt like to you.

Page 88, paragraphs 2 and 3, read aloud.
Page 89, paragraph 1 says:
He was away for two days, during which he refused to take note of the
enemy's attacks.

Do not let the devil get your attention!

As soon as you notice Satan trying to get your attention, or to keep it
focused on bad thoughts, don't let him have it or keep it; get back on a
good track.
1.   List some of the things you can immediately do to get your mind back

from the devil: _____

_____

_____

Page 89, paragraph 2, says: "The next case was harder."
The vital question was: What was God's will?

**The Lord's will
must be revealed
in each case.**

Only the impartial can find God's will.

36

Page 89, last paragraph, to end of chapter, read aloud.
2.   Complete:
      a. God's servant had become _____

      _____

      b. But now, he found that in a moment he could _____

      _____

Christ delivers believers from the power of death.
Read John 3:16, Hebrews 2:14-15.

                    Assignment:
                    List the many ways God has of getting His will across to
                    you: _____

                    _____

                    _____

                    _____

                    _____

                    _____

                    _____

                    _____

                    _____

                    _____

                    _____

                    _____

                    _____

                    _____

Read Chapter 14: A FATHER TO ORPHANS

Page 91, end of first paragraph:
> Rees says, "Blood is thicker than water," and God replies, "Yes, but *spirit* is thicker than blood!"

We are children of God.
Read John 1:12-13, 1 John 3:1-2, Romans 8:16-17, 8:19.

Page 92, paragraph 2, read aloud.
> Rees told God, "You will have to change my nature."

Page 92, paragraph 3, read aloud.

It was the love of God flowing through me.

Discussion Question: Why is it so important to have this kind of love flowing through each one of us?

Page 93, paragraph 2, read aloud.
1. The Lord felt there would be no need to test this position again, unless what two things happened?

   a. _____ b. _____
Discussion Question: What is the meaning of each?

Page 93, paragraph 3, read aloud.
Discussion Question: What does it mean that the Holy Ghost can never "bind the strong man" through us on a higher level than which He has first had victory in us?

Page 94, paragraph 2, says:
> ". . . we cannot say a thing is wrong for others just because we have been called to give it up; it depends on our position or grade in life."

Discussion Question: What are some of the things you no longer do, that you used to do, and that you now condemn in others?

We are not to judge others.
Read Romans 14:1,4,10,13.

We are to judge ourselves first.
Read Matthew 7:1-5.

What would God have us do?
Read Philippians 1:9-11.

It is hard not to judge others; but when you criticize—especially immature Christians, or those just starting to learn about the love of God—you may hurt their feelings, and even their relationship to Jesus . . . by not being a loving representative of God.

> **Let people know you disapprove without being hurtful.**

Page 94, the Lord guided Rees to pay the man's Sick Benefit Club fees.

Page 95, the love of God broke the man down.

Page 95, first partial paragraph, states:
God would keep others through him if he gave perfect obedience to the Holy Spirit.
Discussion Question: How does obedience to the Holy Spirit allow God to keep others through you?

Page 95, paragraph 1, read aloud.
2.   In all these experiences the Lord had a twofold purpose:

    a. _____

    b. _____

Personal Question: How is this happening in your life?

> **The Holy Ghost was judging by the motive.**

Read 1 Corinthians 4:5.

Page 96, first paragraph, Rees mentions that his life "in Christ ... was a life of fullest liberty."

Personal Question: Is your life full of liberty or bondages? List liberties or bondages below:

_____

_____

_____

_____

_____

The devil is the captor.
Read 2 Timothy 2:26.
Christ releases us from all bondages.
Read John 8:34-36, Galatians 5:1, Romans 8:21.
3.   Why does the devil want captives?

_____

Prayer: We ask that the Holy Spirit bring to mind those things that keep us in bondage, and that by the power in the Name of Jesus these things be removed.

Consider this a deliverance, not a loss.

Assignment:
Read Isaiah 61:1-3 and list all the things the Spirit of the Lord is going to do through you:

1.   _____

2.   _____

3.   _____

4.   _____

5.   _____

6.   _____

7.   _____

8.   _____

9. _____

10. _____

a. And what will you be called? _____

_____

b. What will you display? _____

Read Chapter 15: LORD RADSTOCK

Page 97, paragraph 2, read aloud.
1. Complete:

   a. _____ can pray for a thing to be done without necessarily being willing for the answer to come through himself; and he is not even bound to continue in the prayer until it is answered.

   b. _____ is responsible to gain his objective, and he can never be free till he has gained it.

Page 97, last paragraph, read aloud.

> **Self shall take no glory.**

Pride can so easily come. You have to be aware of it, and know that it is only because you have the presence of God that you have His power, and that *all the glory belongs to God!*

2. Look up the word "pride": _____

_____

Read Mark 7:20-23.
3. Where does pride come from? _____

Read Psalm 73:6-8.
4. Referring to the prosperous wicked, what is their necklace? _____

_____

Read Proverbs 16:18, 13:10.
5. What are the results of pride? _____

_____

Personal Question: When there is a quarrel at home, what is usually at the root of it, in you?

42

Read Romans 12:3.
6.   What are God's instructions to us? _____

_____

_____

Read Proverbs 16:5.
7.   What is God's opinion of the prideful? _____

_____

Read Isaiah 25:11-12.
8.   What will be God's judgment on the proud? _____

_____

> **Beware of pride . . .
> especially when walking
> in the gifts of the Spirit.**

Assignment:
Put an "x" next to the statements below which we like to
think show humility but are really prideful:
( ) I'm not worthy.
( ) They don't want me to go.
( ) I'm uncomfortable in their presence.
( ) I don't know how, and am sure I can't learn.
( ) I'll stay home rather than walk with a cane.
( ) Nobody gives to me; why should I give to them?
( ) Open his eyes to your Word, Lord, so he can be good
     like me!
( ) God only uses people walking in the Spirit like me.
Add two of your own:

1. _____

2. _____

Read Chapter 16: CALLED TO A HIDDEN LIFE

Page 101, first paragraph, read aloud.

> **The enemy kept his hold on them.**

Discussion Question: What does this tell you about most bad habits?

Read Matthew 12:29, 16:19.

1. Write a prayer below that would combine these words of God about

    setting the captives free: _____

    _____

    _____

    _____

    _____

> **The only enemy we had
> was the devil himself!**

Page 102, paragraph 1, says: "Oh, how precious the name of Jesus was to us!"

Read Acts 3:6,16.
Discussion Question: What does the name of Jesus mean to you?

Page 102, paragraph 2, read aloud.

2. What does being in an "attitude of prayer" mean to you?

    _____

Page 102, paragraph 3, through paragraph 1 of page 103, read aloud.

44

Discussion Question: How does the world influence you and keep you from walking in the holiness of God?

> **The Lord had asked me to
> keep in an attitude of prayer all day.**

Page 103, paragraphs 2 and 3, read aloud.

> How much of the world is in us,
> when we think we are dead to it!

The Lord will deal with us about seemingly simple things in our lives ... but they could be big blocks in keeping Him from flowing in us the way He wants to.

> **The Holy Ghost would allow no compromise.**

Personal Question: Do I compromise on things I know the Lord has instructed me to do His way, still doing them my way?

Page 104, paragraphs 1 and 2, read aloud.

3. Complete: "It seemed that the _____ had gathered all the

    forces of hell to attack this _____ ."
    If the devil goes that all-out to keep us from obeying the Word of God, then obedience to the Word must be a powerful weapon that will wipe him out!
4. List some of the ways you can wipe Satan out of your life, and keep

    him out. _____

    _____

    _____

Page 104, paragraphs 3 and 4, read aloud.

Page 105, first paragraph, read aloud.
> God was separating Rees to Himself and preparing to take him much farther than this.

Read 2 Corinthians 6:17-18.

Discussion Question: How in certain instances are you the only one who can help save or influence a person that God is trying to get into His Kingdom?

Page 105, paragraphs 2 and 3, read aloud.

> **If my aim in life was to do God's will then I could truly say either way would be equal joy.**

Personal Question: Is my aim in life to do God's will . . . or my will?

Read Matthew 12:50, 1 John 5:14-15.

Page 105, last paragraph, says: "God brought Rees through and made another deep change in his nature."

> **It is God who replaces self with His nature.**

Assignment:
Look back over the past ten years and list some of the changes God has made in you:

_____
_____
_____
_____
_____
_____

So . . . be patient with your loved ones; it took a while for *you* to come around also.

Assignment for during the week:
Keep in an attitude of prayer all day, and write the results here: _____
_____
_____

Read Chapter 17: THE HATLESS BRIGADE

Page 107, paragraph 2, says: The Holy Spirit would always probe down to the very root of the *self* He wanted to get at.

> **The flesh made a hundred and one excuses . . . but the Holy Ghost would have none of them.**

Personal Question: Do I make excuses to God?

Page 108, first paragraph, read aloud.

Read 1 Corinthians 6:17, 12:12-13.
Discussion Question: What does it mean to become one with the Holy Ghost?

Page 108, paragraph 2, says:
The Spirit "who never pushes" drew him with the cords of love.

> **Draw your loved ones in, with cords of love.**

Assignment:
List the cords of love you use:

_____

_____

_____

_____

_____

_____

Read Chapter 18: THE VOW OF A NAZARITE

Page 113, paragraph 2, says:
> It was evident that the Lord had been preparing His servant to gain a much higher position than he had realized, and for this he was going to be turned aside from his work among men . . .
>
> . . . to deal only with God—
> with no means of influence
> except by way of the Throne.

Page 113, last paragraph, read aloud.

> **The Holy Ghost would be his teacher.**

Discussion Question: How does this apply in all the things you do?

1. What does it mean to wait before the Lord? _____

    _____

    _____

Page 114, paragraph 2: Instead of fellowship with Christians, it was to be only with the Lord.

Page 114, last two paragraphs, read aloud.

> **To silence the voices of self**
> **provides**
> **access into the presence of God.**

Discussion Question: What are the voices of self?

Read Psalm 16:11, 1 Chronicles 17:27 (KJV).

48

Page 115, paragraph 1, read aloud.
Now read Isaiah chapter 20 (it is short). Note how specifically God spoke to
Isaiah.

> **The Holy Spirit
> will give you specific
> instructions.**

Page 115, last paragraph, through paragraph 2 of page 116, read aloud.
"If there is no world in you, how can the world influence you?"

Page 116, paragraph 3, read aloud.

> **. . . until the souls of other people
> become to you the same as the
> souls of your own relatives.**

Page 116, paragraph 3, also says:
"He knew he had to go through with it; it was no use kicking against
the pricks. As usual, Rees had to say, 'Pull me through!' "

Page 117, paragraphs 1 and 2, read aloud.

Read Mark 15:5, Isaiah 53:7.

Page 117, last paragraph, read aloud.
2.   What is the only reason Rees Howells did all of these things?

_____

Page 118, last paragraph, read aloud.

> **But if at the beginning
> the world was affecting him,
> by the end
> it was he who was affecting the world . . .
> for people sensed the presence of God with him.**

Page 119, paragraphs 1 and 2, read aloud.

Read 2 Corinthians 4:17-18.

> **It was the process of sanctification,**
> **when the self-nature and all its lusts**
> **had to be changed for the Divine nature.**

Read Romans 6:6-7, 2 Peter 1:4.
3.   Can I see daily progress along these lines? _____

Page 119, paragraph 3, read aloud.
Discussion Question: What is meant by "wonderful liberty in the presence of God"?

Assignment:
Write out two verses that show that a soul is a very precious commodity:

1. _____

_____

_____

_____

_____

2. _____

_____

_____

_____

_____

Read Chapter 19: UNCLE DICK'S HEALING

Page 121, first paragraph, read aloud.

> The fellowship I had had
> with the Lord Himself
> surpassed all I ever had with man!

1. List some of the things that were hardest in your life that have now

    become the sweetest: _____

    _____

Page 122, first paragraph, summary:
When you take the place of another, you take the suffering of another; you
    have to walk every inch of it.

Page 122, paragraphs 4 through 6, read aloud.

> **The point of fasting
> is to bring the body into subjection
> to the Spirit.**

Each fast, if carried out under the guidance of the Holy Spirit, means
that our bodies become more equipped to carry burdens.

Discussion Question: What experiences have you had with fasting?

There are no set rules in the Bible for fasting. A fast can be short or
long. You can give up one item or a whole meal. It must always be
done under the leading and guidance of the Holy Spirit: the reason, the
time, and what is to be given up.

Read Ezra 8:21,23.

2.   Circle items below that pertain to the above Bible verses:

proclaimed   in humbleness   in pride   as a group

as an individual   asking for a safe journey   fasted and prayed

cried in disbelief   God answered

Read Jonah 3:5,8-9.
3.   Rewrite this in modern-day language, pertaining to you:

_____

_____

_____

_____

_____

_____

_____

_____

_____

Results of fasting and repentance:
Read Jonah 3:10.
Personal Question: Would God also do this for your family and nation?

4.   Look up the word "sackcloth": _____

_____

Fasting and prayer for removal of evil spirits and demons.
Read Matthew 17:20-21, Mark 9:28-29.
Discussion Question: What circumstances in your life might need this kind
of prayer, accompanied by fasting?

> **Prayer and fasting
> is the master key
> to the impossible.**

52

Page 123, summary of paragraphs 1 and 2:
> Rees had an uncle that was an invalid and could not walk. One morning the Holy Spirit spoke to him: "It is the Father's will to restore your uncle."

Page 123, paragraphs 3 through 6, read aloud.

Page 124, first paragraph, read aloud.

> It was to be as much of a reality
> to them *then* as it would be to other
> people after it became a fact.

Faith is the realization of things hoped for, the proof of things not seen.
5. Copy Hebrews 11:1 from the Living Bible here:

_____

_____

_____

_____

Page 124, paragraph 3, read aloud.
6. Complete: The Holy Spirit warned them _____ .

    If they did, their _____ .

Page 125, paragraphs 1 and 2, read aloud.
Discussion Question: Relate the sovereignty of God to this situation and similar ones in your life.

Page 125, paragraph 5 to end of chapter, read aloud.

> **Assignment:**
> Explain what part intercession had to do with the healing of Rees' uncle:

_____

_____

_____

_____

_____

Read Chapter 20: CALLED OUT FROM WAGE-EARNING

Page 127, first paragraph, read aloud.

1.   Write in the block below, the most dynamic part of this paragraph:

```
┌─────────────────────────────────────────────┐
│   _____        │
│                                               │
│   _____        │
│                                               │
│   _____        │
└─────────────────────────────────────────────┘
```

Read Genesis 1:26.

We are made in the image of the God who created this universe. He has given us the ability to know Him . . . to be filled with His Spirit . . . to be like Him, and to walk in His *Holy* Spirit. And when you walk in the Spirit, you walk in love.

Some older versions of the Bible use the word "charity" rather than "love." And according to *Unger's Bible Dictionary,* the only Bible word translated "charity" really means "love." *Its absence invalidates all claims to the Christian name.*

Read 1 Corinthians 13:4-5.

2.   List below what love is:

_____

_____

_____

_____

_____

Personal Question: Is that a picture of you?

> When you walk in the Spirit, you *listen* to
> the voice of God.
> When you walk in the Spirit, you *obey*
> the voice of God.

Read Proverbs 8:32-35.

3.   What results are we promised if we listen to and obey God? _____

_____

Discussion Question: What does it mean to receive God's favor?

> When you walk in the Spirit
> you trust and abide in the Lord.

Read Proverbs 3:5-6, Psalm 91:1-2.

4.   Does this mean you rely on God once in a while, or all the time?

_____

Page 127, last paragraph, read aloud.

Page 128, paragraphs 1 through 3, read aloud.
    The Lord was impressing on him that the real life of faith meant
    receiving all that he needed from God.

Page 129, paragraph 1, read aloud.

5.   What did Rees Howells do on his month's vacation? _____

_____

Page 129, paragraph 2 says:
The devil kept bothering him with negative thoughts. The Lord told Rees,
    "Don't allow the devil to speak to you again."
Personal Question: Can you do that? Work at it.

Page 129, paragraph 4 and to the end of the chapter, summary:
    Rees' father was giving him a bad time, on the day before his rent was
    due; and while they were speaking, the postman arrived with a letter
    for Rees. It was from Mr. Gossett, offering him a position in the
    London City Mission, at a salary of 100 pounds a year.

> It was a good beginning to forty
> years of praying and abundantly proving
> the Lord's Prayer: *"Give us this day our daily bread."*

Assignment:
The Lord's Prayer is listed below from the King James

Version; alongside, write it out as a personal letter from
you to God.
Matthew 6:9-13

Our Father   _____

which art in heaven,   _____

hallowed be thy name.   _____

Thy Kingdom come.   _____

Thy will be done in earth,   _____

as it is in heaven.   _____

Give us this day our   _____

    daily bread.   _____

And forgive us our debts,   _____

as we forgive our debtors.   _____

And lead us not into   _____

    temptation,   _____

but deliver us from evil: _____

For thine is the kingdom,   _____

and the power,   _____

and the glory,   _____

    for ever. Amen.   _____

_____

_____

_____

_____

_____

_____

_____

Read Chapter 21: MADEIRA

Page 131, first paragraph, read aloud.

Page 131, last paragraph, read aloud.
Discussion Question: What does he mean, he could only use it as led by the Spirit?

Page 132, paragraph 1, says: "The doctor said he could not possibly live through the winter unless he went to a tropical climate, such as Madeira."

Page 132, paragraphs 2 and 3, read aloud.

Page 132, last paragraph, read aloud.
Personal Question: Can you truly say this is how you treat others: "Do to others as you would they should do to you"?

Page 133, paragraphs 1 through 4, read aloud.

> **Know that when God is leading,**
> **He always has a special purpose in all**
> **He has you do or in what He provides.**

Page 134, paragraph 1, read aloud.
Discussion Question: What does he mean by, "I took care of my mind"?

Page 134, paragraphs 2 and 3, read aloud.
"I brought you to Madeira, to this place, to show you the difference between my love and yours; and to show you that there is something in your nature that I need to rid you of."

Love others
who do something against you.

57

Page 134, last paragraph, read aloud.

> **I could see
> the root of the Savior's
> nature was love, . . .
> and if the root of mine was love,
> nothing the missionary did could affect me.**

Personal Question: Would you like to function like that?
Discussion Question: What kind of results would it produce in your family if you functioned like that?

Page 135, paragraph 1, read aloud.
1. What are the three items he would receive when he gained the position?

   a. _____

   b. _____

   c. _____

Page 135, paragraphs 2 and 3, read aloud.

2. Complete: "But in six weeks _____ , as much as a drunkard is changed when he sees what the Savior has done for him. I

   changed _____ .

> **Oh, that perfect love!**

Personal Question: Can you see how God is working in your life to bring you into that perfect love?
3. Look up the word "love": _____

   _____

Read Matthew 22:37-40.
4. What is the greatest commandment? _____

   _____

   _____

5.   What is the second? _____

_____

Read 1 John 4:16.
6.   What is God? _____ .

7.   If you are His child, what should you be? _____

Read Romans 5:5.
8.   Where does this love come from? _____

Read Ephesians 3:17-20.
9.   In order to be filled with all the fullness of God, what must I be

established in? _____
Discussion Question: How will God's love overcome the world?

Page 136, first partial paragraph, says (regarding his friend Joe):
   "This sickness is not unto death, *but for the glory of God.*"

Page 136, paragraph 1, says regarding hearing the voice of God:
   "As I entered the little train . . . I heard that Voice which I know as
   really as a child knows his father's voice. It said, 'A month today Joe
   will be restored.' *The glory of God came down on the train.*"
Discussion Question: How has the voice of God become more distinct in
   your life since starting this study?

Page 136, paragraph 2, read aloud.

> **When everything of nature and medicine
> had failed, the Lord showed him that
> a higher law was going to operate.**

Page 136, last paragraph, read aloud.
10. Complete: "It has never happened before because of _____ ."

Page 137, paragraph 2, says:
   ". . . God doesn't step in with a spiritual law till the end of the law of
   nature has been reached."

Page 137, paragraph 4, read aloud.

Page 137, last paragraph, read aloud.
> This case needed no prayer. We trusted His word.

Page 138, paragraphs 1-5, and paragraph 1 of page 139, read aloud.

11. Complete: "If you take the healing from Me against _____

    _____ and _____

    _____ , you will have gained a _____
    than in your uncle's healing."

12. "Only a _____ in _____ could make me do it."

13. List some of the things you can do to strengthen yourself to believe

    God's Word against what you see: _____

    _____

    _____

Page 139, paragraph 2, read aloud.

> **The victory of faith.**

Discussion Question: What does that mean?

Page 140, read aloud.

> Sometimes after your greatest
> victories comes a time of testing.

Read Hebrews 11:1.
14. What is faith? _____

    _____

Read Romans 1:17.
15. How do the righteous live? _____

Discussion Question: Can you see by the evidence of people's lives whether
they are living by faith or not? How?

Results of faith: Read Luke 8:10.
16. What are you given? _____

    _____

Discussion Question: How valuable is this knowledge?

60

Assignment:
List three more verses on the results of faith:

1. _____

_____

_____

2. _____

_____

_____

3. _____

_____

_____

Read Chapter 22: MARRIAGE AND MISSIONARY CALL

Page 141, all four paragraphs, read aloud.

1. What is the most dynamic section of these paragraphs? _____

    _____

    _____

    _____

Page 143, first four paragraphs, read aloud.

2. Complete:

    a. What a privilege to proclaim the _____

    _____

    b. There is no glory like that of proclaiming _____

    c. I was called to preach more about _____

3. Write below: What the results will be in a person's life when he
    believes in eternal life through Christ.

    _____

    _____

    _____

Page 143, last paragraph, through the first three paragraphs of page 144, in
summary says:

> Then, in the midst of all this, God called again. "I walked straight into
> the meeting, and there I saw a vision of Africa! ... The Lord gave me a
> vision of them, and they stood before me as sheep without a
> shepherd."

Page 144, last two paragraphs, read aloud.

4. Look up the word "excuse": _____

    _____

Read Luke 14:16-21.

5.   What did the Master do after all the above excuses? _____

_____

Personal Question: What do you think is God's attitude toward some of your excuses to Him?

Page 145, first four paragraphs, read aloud.

> Prove to me that
> you love the souls of the Africans
> who are to live for eternity
> more than you love your own son.

Page 146, paragraphs 1 and 2, read aloud.
Discussion Question: What did he mean by "we wouldn't have dared to interfere"?

> **When you take your hands off,
> the Lord can move
> in perfection.**

Page 146, paragraph 5, says:
> "We were coming up to the victory by degrees; the process was slow and hard. Because it was going to be an intercession, one had to walk every inch."

Read Philippians 4:13.
6.   Who is your strength? _____

Page 146, last paragraph, through paragraph 1 of page 147, read aloud.

> **Giving our best to the Lord.**

Page 147, paragraph 2, read aloud.

> When you give something up,
> you are *sacrificing*.
> Sacrifice (amplified beyond Webster's definition):

"Giving up something of value to obtain
something of greater value!"

Read Ephesians 5:2.

Assignment:
List things you have given up as sacrifices. Then list what
you have received of a much greater value:

Sacrifice: _____

Received: _____

Sacrifice: _____

Received: _____

Sacrifice: _____

Received: _____

Read Chapter 23: STANDING IN THE QUEUE

Page 149, first three paragraphs, read aloud.
1.   How can you share in a harvest? _____

_____

Page 149, last paragraph, read aloud.
2.   Complete: There is nothing in the world better for strengthening one's

faith than _____ .

Page 150, paragraphs 1 and 2, read aloud.
Personal Question: What is your school of faith?

Read 1 Peter 5:7.

Page 151, last paragraph, and paragraph 1 of page 152, read aloud.

> **It depends wholly on guidance.**

Read Isaiah 58:11-12.
3.   What two names will the one be called who does this:

   a. _____

   b. _____

Page 152, paragraphs 2 and 3, read aloud.
       When we have a very hard thing to do, the Lord will burden us in
       another way to make the former one easier!
Discussion Question: Can anyone give an example of this?

Page 152, last paragraph, read aloud.
Discussion Question: What does it mean: "Our extremity would be God's
       opportunity"?

Page 153, paragraphs 1 through 4, read aloud—with awesome respect for
       the hand of God and its perfect movements!

4. Complete:

   a. It was most _____ ,

   b. and only a _____

   c. of what the Lord would do in Africa, if we would _____ .

Read Exodus 19:5-6.
5. If you like Israel are obedient, what will you be to God?

   _____

   _____

Read 1 Samuel 15:22.
6. What does God desire rather than sacrifice? _____

Read Isaiah 1:18-20.
7. If you are willing and obedient, what happens?

   _____

8. If you resist and rebel, what will happen?

   _____

Read Romans 5:19.
9. Through the obedience of one man I have been made righteous. Who

   was that one man? _____

Read Hebrews 5:8-9.
10. Complete: Jesus learned _____ from what He suffered.

11. Jesus is the source of eternal salvation for all who _____
    Him.
Discussion Question: Do these verses teach salvation by works?

Page 154, paragraph 1, read aloud.
Discussion Question: Has anyone ever had a similar experience?

Page 154, last paragraph, read aloud.

> **Knowing that the One who had
> called them into this life
> was able to deliver
> in all circumstances.**

Assignment:
Write a dynamic prayer, asking the Father to help you
obtain a faith like Rees Howells had standing in that
queue.

_____

_____

_____

_____

_____

_____

_____

_____

_____

_____

_____

_____

_____

Read Chapter 24: REVIVALS IN AFRICA

Page 155 and page 156, paragraph 1, summary:
> The South Africa General Mission had been founded in 1889 to take the gospel into the many unevangelized areas of South Africa.... The Howells were sent to the Rusitu Mission Station in Gazaland, near the border of Portuguese East Africa (now Mozambique).

> **The source of all revival is the Holy Ghost.**

In the meetings that Mr. Howells took he continued to speak to them about revival, and in six weeks the Spirit began to move upon the Christians.

1.   Look up the word "revive": _____

_____

Read Isaiah 57:15, Hosea 6:2-3.
2.   What is the reason God is reviving and restoring us? _____

_____

Discussion Question: What does this mean to you?

Page 156, paragraph 2, through paragraph 1 of page 157, read aloud.

> **Heaven had opened,
> and there was no room
> to contain the blessing.**

Page 157, last paragraph, through paragraph 1 of page 158:
> Truly "sowing in tears" the seed of life with patience and prayer....
> The Spirit doing a mighty convicting work in souls and leading to confessions such as no human agency could have extorted from them.

67

Page 158, last paragraph, read aloud.
3. Complete: This was done without any _____ under the

    _____ .

Page 159, last paragraph, through paragraph 1 of page 160, read aloud.
4. By what can we fan the flames of revival into a mighty blaze? ____

    _____

Page 160, paragraphs 2 and 3, read aloud.
    "I was pleading on His word. . . ."
Read Malachi 3:10.

Page 161, paragraph 2, read aloud.

> **They were so full of joy.**

Page 161, last paragraph, read aloud.

> **The Holy Ghost was going in us,**
> **and He is the Author of Pentecost**
> **and the Source of revival.**

Page 162, paragraphs 2 through 4, read aloud.
Discussion Question: What can a dynamic testimony do? Why?

Page 163, paragraph 2:

> **On the third day, the power that was there!**
> **It wasn't the preaching;**
> **it was the power!**

Discussion Question: How is the Holy Spirit your power source?

Page 164, paragraph 3, read aloud.
Read Zechariah 4:6.

Page 166, paragraph 2, read aloud.

5. Write out Romans 8:28: _____

_____

_____

_____

_____

Get this into your spirit, and when things go wrong, repeat it to yourself!

Page 166, last paragraph, read aloud.

> **You didn't ask believing.**

Page 167, last paragraph, on to page 168, says:
> The witch doctors have failed and
> the ancestral spirits have failed—
> but our God has not failed.

Read Deuteronomy 31:8.

6. Write this out in your own words, pertaining to you:

_____

_____

_____

_____

_____

Page 168, paragraph 2, read aloud.

> **The Holy Ghost
> was stronger than death.**

Discussion Question: How can knowing the above help in future times of tribulation?

Page 168, paragraph 3, read aloud.
> Rees Howells said, "How I praised God for my personal Guide!"

7. Who is this personal Guide? _____

70

8.   Is He available to you? _____

List below some of the things He has recently guided you into or through:

_____

_____

_____

_____

Page 169, first paragraph, read aloud.
"Don't you believe that I can keep the germ from overcoming you?"

> **I found the Holy Spirit in me was stronger than the flu.**

Read Psalm 91:1-7.
Discussion Question: How are your body and mind protected by the indwelling Holy Spirit?

Page 169, paragraphs 2 and 3, read aloud.
"So I brought them before the Lord, and pleaded His Word."

The news spread that the God of the white man was stronger than death.

In order to receive the promises of God they had to work in faith and obedience ... and do exactly as God told them.

Read 2 Timothy 1:1.

Page 171, last paragraph, read aloud.
"I don't think we had anything to cause us an hour's trouble, and for both my wife and myself, they were the six happiest years of our lives."

9.   How could anyone say they weren't caused any trouble ... with all the

sickness going on around them? _____

_____

71

Assignment:
Meditation, and the Power of the Spirit
Joshua 1:8 "Do not let this Book of the Law depart from your mouth; meditate on it day and night, so that you may be careful to do everything written in it. Then you will be prosperous and successful."
Results of Meditation
Jeremiah 33:3 "Call to me and I will answer you and tell you great and unsearchable things you do not know."

Instructions:
Sit quietly before the Lord your God. Know that He is God, your heavenly Father. Worship and adore Him.
Read this verse from Zechariah:
Zechariah 4:6 " 'Not by might nor by power, but by my Spirit,' says the Lord Almighty."
Meditate on the above verses.
Ask the Lord to tell you great and unsearchable things you do not know—to show you on the "television screen of your mind" what He wants you to know.

Write on the lines below what He has revealed to you:

_____

_____

_____

_____

_____

_____

_____

_____

_____

_____

Read Chapter 25: BUYING THE FIRST ESTATE IN WALES

Page 173, last paragraph, through paragraph 2 of page 174, read aloud.

Read 1 Chronicles 28:20-21.

Page 174, paragraph 3, says:
> The Lord told them that they would have to do it by faith.

Discussion Question: Has the Lord ever told you that?

Page 175, paragraphs 3 and 4, read aloud.
1.   Complete:
     a. They gave themselves ————————————————————
     b. to be ———————————————— to raise up a college.
     c. They knew it was a ———————————————— .

Personal Question: Are you an instrument of God?

Page 175, last paragraph, says:
> They had no idea where the College was to be. Like Abraham, they
> went out not knowing whither they went. "The moment we went to
> Mumbles [a seaside village near the city of Swansea], I knew it was the
> place where God wanted us to be."

Page 176, paragraph 1, read aloud.
2.   What did God say to them? ————————————————
     ————————————————————————————

Page 176, paragraph 2, read aloud.
3.   What did God say to them? ————————————————

Personal Question: Can you hear God's voice like that?

Read Hebrews 1:1-2 (LB).
4.   How does God speak to us today? ———————————————

Read Revelation 3:20.
5.   What happens when we listen? ————————————————
     ————————————————————————————

Read John 8:47.
6.   Who cannot hear God? _____

_____

Page 177, first paragraph, read aloud.
7.   What would Rees have to do if the proof came?

a. _____

b. _____

Read Psalm 37:5-6, 1 Timothy 6:12.
Personal Question: Can you apply these two verses to your life right now?

Page 177, paragraph 3, read aloud.

Page 178, paragraph 2, read aloud.

Page 180, paragraphs 1 through 4, read aloud.

> **I came to the place where I knew that whenever God wants to take over a property, the owner had very little to do with it!**

Write below how that principle could apply in your everyday life:

_____

_____

_____

_____

Page 181, paragraphs 1 and 2, read aloud.
8.   We seem to be affected by anything anybody says or does. Why?

> **Once you have heard His voice, know He is in charge!**

Page 181, paragraph 3, read aloud.

74

Discussion Question: Discuss God's perfect abilities and timing.

Page 181, last paragraph, read aloud.

> **His eyes were to be on God alone.**

Read 2 Chronicles 20:12.
> God promised him the money, but Rees had to pray it in.

Personal Question: Can you visualize the miraculous results in your life if you could touch on this kind of communion with God?

Page 182, paragraph 2, talks about the Book of Haggai.
Read Haggai 2:8.

> God is our Provider.

Read Psalm 37:3-7.
9. What are you told to do? _____

_____

10. If I delight myself in the Lord, what will He give me?

_____

11. And when I commit my way to Him? _____

_____

_____

12. In verse 7, what am I told to do? _____

_____

Page 182, paragraphs 3 and 4, read aloud.

Page 183, paragraphs 1 and 2, read aloud.
Discussion Question: What was it that allowed God to work on behalf of getting Rees the money he needed?

> **The moment he believed, God moved.**

Page 183, paragraphs 3 through 5, read aloud.

It was a serious temptation
to take the easy way of deliverance.

Discussion Question: Can you give some examples of this in your own life?

Page 184, paragraphs 3 through 6, read aloud.

Assignment:
List six things in your life that would not have happened
without prayer:

1. _____

2. _____

3. _____

4. _____

5. _____

6. _____

Read Chapter 26: THE BIBLE COLLEGE OF WALES

Page 185, first paragraph, read aloud.
1.   Look up the word "fire" in a Bible Dictionary: _____

_____

Read Matthew 3:11.

Page 185, paragraph 2, says: "The Lord warned him that trouble was coming, but that through it He would purge the work, to His own glory."

Read Malachi 3:2-3.
Discussion Question: What has been the process of your refinement?

Page 186, paragraph 2, read aloud.

> The College was put on
> the Rock of Ages.

Personal Question: Can you put your life on that same Rock?

> When we are on the foundation of
> Jesus Christ, no man nor devil
> can shake it.

Read Hebrews 12:26-27.
Discussion Question: What in your life has been shaken, what is being shaken, and what cannot be shaken?

On pages 186 and 187 is a report issued on the fifth anniversary of the College.
Read Proverbs 3:5-6.

Below are listed seven highlights of this report. On the line underneath, write what the Lord tells you regarding your own personal circumstances.

1. Accomplished through faith and believing prayer.

   _____

2. No appeal was to be made for finance.

   _____

3. Visible proof that He is the living and faithful God.

   _____

4. It has been the Father's will to teach us the way to trust Him each morning for the day's needs.

   _____

5. The Lord has been proving to us day by day that "living faith" is above circumstances.

   _____

6. We were allowed to be tested beyond our strength.

   _____

7. We should not trust in ourselves._____

   _____

> **Assignment:**
> Write a praise paragraph, thanking the Lord for being so faithful to you in all circumstances:
>
> _____
>
> _____
>
> _____
>
> _____
>
> _____
>
> _____
>
> _____
>
> _____
>
> _____
>
> _____

Read Chapter 27: BUYING THE SECOND ESTATE

Page 189, first paragraph, read aloud.

Page 190, paragraph 1, first two sentences, read aloud.

Page 190, paragraph 2, read aloud.
> The Lord always shows you all the difficulties when He is going to do anything through you.

Discussion Question: Can anyone give an example of this?
Personal Question: Can you praise before the victory?

Page 191, paragraphs 3 and 4, read aloud.
> We read that many vain imaginations were placed in Rees Howells' mind by the devil. It is not good to let our imaginations run away. It can cause our spirits to be depressed and not usable to God.

Read Romans 1:21 (KJV).
1. What happened to their heart? _____

Read 2 Corinthians 10:5.
2. What did Rees Howells do to the devil's arguments and what are we

   supposed to do when he comes at us like this? _____

_____

Page 191, last paragraph, through paragraph 2 of page 192, read aloud.

The Word of God is trustworthy and true.

Read Psalm 111:7-8, 119:142,151,160.

Page 193, paragraphs 1-5, read aloud.

Page 194, last paragraph, read aloud.

Assignment:
Write out three Bible verses on the Faithfulness of God.

1. _____

_____

_____

_____

_____

2. _____

_____

_____

_____

_____

3. _____

_____

_____

_____

_____

Read Chapter 28: THIRD ESTATE AND CHILDREN'S HOME

Page 195, first paragraph, read aloud.

Page 195, paragraph 2, says:

> "The Lord kept me daily and hourly
> abiding
> to fulfill the condition for claiming
> an answer to my prayers."

Personal Question: Do you abide, moment by moment, in the Lord's presence?

Page 195, last paragraph, read aloud.

Page 196, paragraphs 3 and 4, read aloud.
1.   Complete: Out of the travail came the _____ of the Home and School for missionaries' children.

Page 197, paragraphs 1 through 3, read aloud.
Discussion Question: Talk about how the hand of the Lord moves before His children.

Page 197, paragraph 4, first sentence, read aloud.

> You are always getting a death on a
> point that is not really essential,
> and then receiving a better thing for it.

Read Psalm 40:1-3, 2 Corinthians 4:17-18, Romans 8:18-19.
Discussion Question: Can anyone give a personal example of having received something better after having something you thought was good taken away?

Page 198, paragraph 2, read aloud.
2.   Complete: a. He would regard a temporary disappointment en route

not as a failure but as a _____ —

b. ... like a climber who scales a peak mistakenly thinking

it is the summit, only to find _____

c. ... and to find his _____ increased to
reach it.

> **Not a failure
> but
> a stepping stone.**

List some of your recent stepping stones: _____

_____

Page 198, last paragraph, through paragraph 1 of page 199, summary:
The Bible College at this time had about fifty students. The school for
missionaries' children opened in 1933, with eleven boys and girls,
including some day pupils from the surrounding district who were also
accepted.

Page 199, paragraphs 2 and 3, read aloud.

He believed the law of the hundredfold, and acted on it.

Assignment:
Read the following verses on the Hundredfold, and write
next to each one the point or points that stand out to you:

Genesis 26:12 _____

_____

Matthew 13:23 _____

_____

Mark 10:29-30 _____

_____

Luke 8:8 _____

_____

Read Chapter 29: THE BOOK OF COMMON PRAYER AND KING EDWARD VIII

Page 201, first paragraph, read aloud.
1.   What two types of prayer were mentioned?

a. _____ b. _____

Page 201, paragraphs 2 through 4, read aloud.
Discussion Question: What did it mean: "The Lord had given us the victory the previous afternoon"?

Page 202, paragraph 1, read aloud.

Pages 202-203, summary of the account from "The Diaries of the Daily Meetings."
(As you read this summary, compare it to what has happened in your life, is happening, or will happen; and use it as a parallel . . . to know how God will respond.)
1. The conditions are serious.
2. We plead with the Lord to guide the king, give him wisdom.
3. Day of Prayer . . . situation very grave.
4. Day of Prayer and Fasting.
5. The Lord reveals that it is His will for Edward to abdicate.
6. Thanksgiving over the victory.
7. The King is now anxious to do what is best for the Empire.
8. We trust the Lord to help the king make the decision according to God's will.
9. The news of King Edward VIII's abdication becomes known.
10. We ask the Lord to control the country.
11. We are thankful for this believing of the Holy Spirit.
Discussion Question: What does "the believing of the Holy Spirit" mean?

Page 203, paragraphs 6 and 7, read aloud.

Assignment: Regarding Giving and Receiving.
Read the following verses and write beside them that

82

which the Lord wants you to give forth, and what He wants to give back to you:

Malachi 3:8-10

Give: _____

Receive: _____

Luke 6:38

Give: _____

Receive: _____

Philippians 4:17

Give: _____

Receive: _____

Read Chapter 30: THE EVERY CREATURE COMMISSION

Page 205, first paragraph, read aloud.

Results of being in God's presence:
Read Psalm 139:17-18.
1.   When you are in God's presence, what do you obtain? _____

_____

Read Psalm 143:8-10.
2.   (verse 10) When you are in God's presence, He teaches you to

_____.

3.   God's good Spirit leads you _____.

4.   State what the last answer means in your own words: _____

_____.

Page 205, paragraphs 2 and 3, read aloud.

Read Mark 16:15.
5.   This is the beginning of Jesus' last statement before He went to sit at
     the right hand of the Father. Explain how important these words are:

_____

_____

Personal Question: How do these last words pertain to you?

> **Someone has to obey
> and pray out the laborers.**

Read Psalm 2:8, Matthew 9:37-38.
     Note the word "ask," which is the same as "pray."

Page 206, paragraphs 2 through 4, read aloud.

Page 207, first paragraph, read aloud.

6.   Complete: a. As really as the Savior came down to the world to

make _____ ,

b. so the Holy Ghost had come down to make that atone-

ment _____ .

Discussion Question: How do you see this being done, even now?

Page 207, paragraph 2, read aloud.

7.   It is stated that "the College became a house of prayer for all nations."
List the three kinds of prayer targets mentioned:

a. _____

b. _____

c. _____

List the kinds and varieties of prayers you think the Lord would have

you to use in your daily devotions: _____

_____

_____

Page 207, paragraphs 3 and 4, read aloud.

There was prayer warfare on anything
that affected world evangelization.

**God was preparing
an instrument —
a company to fight world battles
on their knees.**

Page 207, paragraph 5, read aloud.

"Prevail Against Hitler."
It meant three weeks of prayer and fasting.

Discussion Question: Talk about what you could obtain for national and
worldwide revival by three weeks of prayer and fasting.

86

Page 208, Diary summary:
1. We ask the Lord to deal with Germany.
2. We plead with God to deal with Hitler.
3. Situation is very black.
4. The Lord is allowing us to plead the "Every Creature Vision" in His presence.
5. The Lord turns our eyes off the countries to Himself.

Discussion Question: Discuss point number 5.

Page 208, paragraph 4, read aloud.
Read Ezekiel 22:30.
Personal Question: Are you this person?

> "I knew from that time on, Hitler was no more
> than a rod in the hands of the Holy Spirit."

Page 208, read aloud: March 30. "Fire fell on sacrifice. . . ."

Read Leviticus 9:22-24.
8.   Write in your own words what this passage means: _____

_____

_____

_____

Page 209, paragraphs 2 and 3, read aloud.

> **It was essentially a clash of spiritual forces —
> a test of strength between the devil in Hitler
> and the Holy Ghost in His army of intercessors.**

Discussion Question: Bring the above statement down to everyday terms in regard to your local and family circumstances.

Page 209, paragraphs 4 through 6, read aloud.

Pages 209 and 210, summary:
> The reason war had been averted for the moment
> was that Hitler for the first time failed to obey *his
> voice.* . . . "The Lord had 'bent' Hitler."

Read Isaiah 60:14.

Page 210, last paragraph, read aloud.

Assignment:
List things below you would like to see bow before the
Lord:

_____

_____

_____

_____

_____

_____

_____

_____

_____

_____

Read Chapter 31: ETHIOPIA

Page 211, first paragraph, says:
>   Soon after the crisis of March 1936 came the
>   fight for Ethiopia. It was hard and long, and
>   seemed to end in dismal failure.

Page 211, paragraph 3:
1.   Complete: The battle of intercession lasted for three weeks. It was

as if _____

_____ .

Page 212, paragraph 6, read aloud.
>   "The death in an intercession
>   which has to precede the
>   resurrection."

2.   They were told to walk through their valley of humiliation, of

apparent failure, with what? _____

3.   Apparent failure may only be a stepping stone to what? _____

_____

Read Romans 4:20-21.

Page 214, partial paragraph at top, gives an Ethiopian proverb:
>   "The man who has only God to look to can do all things and never
>   fail."

Read Philippians 4:13 (KJV).

Page 215, last paragraph, read aloud:
>   God's answer was perfect.

Read Psalm 20:4-7.
Discussion Question: Discuss the above psalm, verse by verse.

89

Assignment:
Write some of the perfections of God that appeal to you:

_____

_____

_____

_____

_____

_____

_____

_____

_____

(Remember, you are His offspring.)

Read Chapter 32: VISITATION OF THE SPIRIT

Page 217, paragraph 1, first 3 sentences, read aloud.

> They laid their lives on the altar
> as intercessors.

Read Genesis 8:20.
1.   Complete: The altar was a place of _____ .

Read Exodus 30:1,7-8.
2.   Complete: The altar was a place for _____ .

Read Exodus 29:12.
3.   Complete: The altar is a place where the _____ is applied.

Read Leviticus 6:13.
4.   Complete: The fire must be kept burning on the altar _____

_____ .

> A body with one life and one purpose.

Read Romans 15:6.

Page 217, paragraph 2, says:
> There was an increasing consciousness of God's presence. They wept before Him for hours, broken at the corruption of their own hearts revealed in the light of His holiness.

Discussion Question: Discuss what the holiness of God means to you.

5.   Look up "holiness of God" in a Bible Dictionary _____

_____

_____

6.   Look up "holiness of man" in a Bible Dictionary _____

_____

Read 1 Peter 1:16, Revelation 4:8.
7.   Write below: Why God wants His children to be holy.

_____

_____

Page 217, last paragraph, through paragraph 2 of page 218, read aloud.

> The person of the Holy Ghost
> filled all our thoughts,
> His light penetrated all the hidden
> recesses of our hearts.

Personal Question: Have you felt like this recently?

Page 218, paragraphs 3 and 4, read aloud.

8.   Fill in: It was not so much _____ we saw as _____ . We saw _____ and _____ underlying everything we had ever done. _____ and _____ were discovered in places where we had never suspected them. . . . In His nature He [the Holy Ghost] was _____ — He would never _____ _____ , but always _____ .

**"There is all the difference
in the world between *your* surrendered
life in My hands,
and Me living *My* life in your body."**

Page 219, paragraph 1, read aloud.
The Holy Ghost as a divine Person lived in the bodies of the apostles.
Read Acts 4:8, Acts 7:55, Acts 13:9.
9.   List who the person was in each verse that was indwelt by the Holy

Spirit: a. _____ b. _____ c. _____ .

10.   On page 219, the Holy Spirit asked what two things of them?

a. _____ b. _____

Read Romans 12:1.

> How much there was in us

that still wanted
to live our own lives!

Read Luke 9:24.

11. Rewrite the above verse in your own words, as it pertains to you.

_____

_____

_____

Page 219, paragraph 4, read aloud.

There was a work to be done in the world today
that only the Holy Spirit could do.

Read John 16:8.

12. What does the Holy Spirit convict people of? _____

_____

_____

> **The Holy Spirit is as almighty
> as He is holy.**

Page 220, paragraph 1, read aloud.

So that I may live in your body for the sake of a lost world.

Read Colossians 3:3, 2 Corinthians 4:10, Galatians 2:20.
Discussion Question: What does all this mean to you personally?

Page 220, paragraph 2, read aloud.

13. Complete the following:

a. _____ would never be able to hold out.

b. The final contest between _____ for the

kingdoms of _____ .

c. We could see only One Person who was _____ for
these things.

d. And He was the _____ of the

Godhead, in those whom He was _____ .

Personal Question: Are you that person?

Discussion Question: How does all this relate to what is going on in the
Christian and non-Christian world right now?

Page 220, paragraph 3, says:
> The wonder of our privilege overwhelmed us.

Page 220, last paragraph, read aloud.

> He had come and He could never fail.

Discussion Question: What does he mean by "bringing our experience up to the level of His Word"?

Page 221, paragraph 1, read aloud.

> **You have come
> to shake the world.**

Read Isaiah 2:19, 13:13, Ezekiel 38:20, Joel 3:16, Haggai 2:6-7, Hebrews 12:26.

Personal Question: Are you becoming that one that cannot be shaken?

Page 221, last paragraph, says:
> Recognize His mighty working
> in and through others.

> **The Holy Spirit is going to
> fulfill prophecy through His prepared channels
> in all parts of the world.**

Page 222, read aloud.

> One body for one God-appointed purpose.

> **Assignment:**
> Look up in a variety of dictionaries the word "shake" and list the meanings below:
>
> _____
>
> _____
>
> _____
>
> _____
>
> _____

Read Chapter 33: FOURTH ESTATE AND THE JEWS

Page 223, first paragraph, read aloud.

> **No great event in history,
> even though prophesied, comes to pass
> unless God finds His human channels of
> faith and obedience.**

Page 223, paragraph 3, read aloud.

Page 224, paragraph 1, says: "I firmly believe the times of the Gentiles are drawing to a close, and the Jews must be back in their own land when the Master returns."

Read Luke 21:24.
1. Look up the word "Gentile": _____

_____ .

Read Jeremiah 16:15.
Page 224, paragraph 2, says:
    "Now God is calling us to be responsible for the Jews."

Page 224, paragraphs 3 and 4, read aloud.

> **Unless the Holy Spirit in you
>   Makes the suffering your own,
> You can't intercede for them;
>   You will never touch the Throne.**

Page 225, paragraph 4, read aloud.

Read 1 Thessalonians 5:16-18.

Page 225, paragraph 5, read aloud.
2.   Whom did Rees Howells say he had to look to, to be his Company?

_____

Page 226, paragraph 1, read aloud.

Page 227, last paragraph, read aloud.

> **God's army of the Spirit**

Read Ephesians 6:12, Joel 2:11, 3:9.

Page 229, paragraph 2, read aloud.
Read Exodus 19:5-6.
3.   Look up the word "covenant": _____

_____

Page 229, paragraphs 3 and 4, read aloud.

Page 230, paragraph 1, read aloud.

The State of Israel was a fact.

Page 230, paragraphs 2 and 3, read aloud and discuss.

Assignment:
Write what you think God's covenant is with you:

_____

_____

_____

_____

(As you read the Bible daily, keep this covenant in mind
when you come across the promises of God.)

Read Chapter 34: INTERCESSION FOR DUNKIRK

Page 231, first paragraph, read aloud.

Page 231, paragraph 2, says:
"Mr. Howells began to see clearly that Hitler was Satan's agent for preventing the gospel going to every creature."
Discussion Question: Discuss how that is still true now, regarding Satan's agents.

Page 232, paragraphs 2 through 4, read aloud.

Page 233, paragraph 2:
1.   What was the dynamic prophetic statement regarding Stalin? _____

_____

_____

Page 233, paragraph 3, read aloud.
2.   Complete: We . . . have to cry out to God in our _____

for _____ .

Page 233, last paragraph, read aloud.

Page 234, paragraphs 1 through 4, read aloud.

Page 235, first two lines, says:
        "It has been a battle between the
        Holy Spirit and the devil which
        we have been fighting for four years."

Page 235, paragraph 1, read aloud.
        "Death in the eyes of the world is victory to the Holy Ghost."

Read 1 Corinthians 15:36, John 12:24, 1 Peter 1:23.

> **The Lord has made very plain**
> **that the victory is from Him and**
> **no one else,**
> **and He is to have all the glory.**

Page 235, last sentence:
3.   Complete: God gets at the enemy _____ and _____ .
Discussion Question: What does that mean?

Page 236, paragraph 2, read aloud.

Page 236, last paragraph, says:
     "The delay has not changed our faith a bit."
     Continue on in this paragraph, starting with, "I feel tonight. . . ."
     Read aloud.

> **If you have faith, you can leave it**
> **in His hands, and He will intervene**
> **at the right time.**

Page 237, paragraphs 4 through 6, read aloud.
Put your personal comment under each statement below:
4.   You do not know how much faith is needed.

5.   Our eyes are on Him today.

6.   Unless He intervenes, we are lost.

7.   Man would not be able to end this.

8.   "Don't expect Me to do it until you get to your extremity."

9.   In the darkest hour.

Page 238, paragraphs 3 and 4, read aloud.

98

10. What was the only reason they were not in a panic? _____

11. _____
    What did they have to do until God did the big thing? _____
    _____

Discussion Question: How were they keeping the enemy in check?
Personal Question: How do you keep the enemy in check?

Page 238, paragraph 7, read aloud.

Can we take the answer?

Page 239, paragraphs 4 and 5, read aloud.
Read the following statement, then close your eyes and visualize what it
    means:
> "The battle is the Holy Spirit's. See Him
> outside yourself tonight; He is there on
> the battlefield with His drawn sword."

Discussion Question: What meaning have you come up with and what have
    you seen?

Page 239, paragraphs 6 and 7, read aloud.

> God had a company of hidden intercessors whose
> lives were on the altar day after day as they stood in
> the gap for the deliverance of Britain.

Assignment:
List the intercessions God has assigned to you:

1. _____
2. _____
3. _____
4. _____
5. _____
6. _____
7. _____

Read Chapter 35: THE BATTLE OF BRITAIN

Page 241, first paragraph, read aloud.

Page 241, paragraph 2, starting with "Must we have fear...?" read aloud.
1. Must you have fear because others have fear? _____
2. Can we trust Him for the impossible? _____

Read Joshua 1:5, Psalm 57:1.

Page 242, paragraph 1, read aloud.

Page 242, paragraph 2, read aloud.

Page 242, last paragraph, read aloud.

Page 243, paragraph 1, read aloud.
The peace the Savior gives is not an artificial one. It is so deep that even the devil can't disturb it.

> **You can't take a shade
> of fear into
> the presence of God.**

Read Isaiah 8:11-13, John 14:27, Philippians 4:7.

Page 243, paragraph 4, read aloud.
He has found believing in us.

Read 2 Timothy 1:12.

Page 243, last paragraph, read aloud.

> **When you believe,
> you finish with prayer.**

100

Discussion Question: What does it mean, "How could we get victory for the world unless we had first believed it for ourselves?"

Page 244, paragraph 1, read aloud.

3. Complete the following: The Holy Ghost has found _____

_____ to what He wants to do.

4. Take care you are _____ . Believing is the most delicate

thing you can think of. It is like a _____ .

5. He couldn't do it before without _____ .

Discussion Question: Talk about the delicate vapor of what your "believing" is.

Page 244, paragraph 4, read aloud.

Page 244, last paragraph, read aloud.

6. Complete: Because _____ , God has made known to us what is to come to pass. List what they are:

a. _____

b. _____

c. _____

Page 245, read aloud.

Assignment:
Explain how the power of God is able to be released onto this earth:

_____

_____

_____

_____

_____

_____

_____

Read Chapter 36: RUSSIA, NORTH AFRICA, ITALY, "D" DAY

Page 247, paragraphs 1 through 3, read aloud.

Page 247, paragraph 4, through paragraph 3 of page 249, read aloud.
Discussion Question: What does it mean, "The prayer was so far beyond us, yet the Spirit laid it on us"?

Page 249, last paragraph through paragraph 1 of page 250, read aloud.
1.   Where were their prayers now to be centered? _____
2.   What three areas are they? a. _____ b. _____
     c. _____

Page 250 paragraph 2, read aloud.

Page 250, paragraph 3, says:

> These Bible lands must be
> protected, because it is to these lands
> the Savior will come back.

Page 251, paragraph 2, read aloud.

Page 251, paragraph 4, through paragraph 3 of page 252, read aloud.

> The hand of Almighty God is in evidence once more.

Read Ezra 8:31, 1 Peter 5:6-7.
Discussion Question: How is God's hand even now on you, your family, and the nations?

Page 252, paragraph 4, through paragraph 2 of page 253, read aloud.

> We found the enemy
> was giving way before us.

101

Page 253, paragraph 3, read aloud.

Personal Question: What has to be done in your life in order for God to be able to pray through you like He did through those in the college?

Read Joel 2:12-13.

Special prayer: "Lord, purge my heart of all uncleanness ... show me Your will and Your way ... make my paths straight. In Jesus' name."

Page 254, paragraph 1, through paragraph 1 of page 255, read aloud.

Confirmed the guidance of the Spirit.

Read John 16:13, 1 Corinthians 2:10-13.

Page 255, paragraph 3, says:
"We have a perfect right to ask God to come and fight with our young men."

Discussion Question: Why did they have a "right" to ask God to do this?

Page 255, last paragraph, through paragraph 1 of page 256, read aloud.

Page 257, paragraphs 1 and 2, read aloud.

Assignment:
List the things you are doing that "every creature might hear the gospel":

_____

_____

_____

_____

_____

_____

_____

Read Chapter 37: HOME CALL

Page 259, first paragraph, read aloud.

Page 259, paragraphs 2 and 3, read aloud.

> **Every creature will
> hear the gospel,
> and the King will come back!**

Page 260, paragraph 2, read aloud.
1.   Complete: The Holy Ghost would _____ in the future to

_____ and reach every creature with

the gospel in _____ .

Page 260, last paragraph, read aloud.

Page 261, paragraph 1, says:
Rees Howells had been faithful in the hands of God in laying the
foundation.

Personal Question: Have you been faithful in doing what God has asked you
to do?

Page 262, paragraphs 1 through 3, read aloud.

Page 262, last paragraph, read aloud.
Discussion Question: What allows the marvelous presence of God to be
present at the departure of a godly man?

Page 263, paragraphs 1 and 2, read aloud.

The College and School still have the
same Guide, Enabler, and Supplier — the Lord Himself!

103

Assignment: (If this is your last session, do this assignment aloud in class.)

Read the following verses and answer the questions regarding life and death:

Ephesians 6:11-12.
1. Who is the enemy of life? _____

Luke 13:16.
2. Who keeps people in bondage? _____

John 8:44.
3. The devil is a _____ and a _____ .

John 3:16.
4. What do we receive from Jesus? _____

Hebrews 2:14-15.
5. Jesus became human and died that He might do what?

_____

_____

2 Timothy 1:10.
6. The appearing of Jesus has done what?

_____

7. And brought what to light? _____

_____

CONCLUSION

If in a group, let each person answer these questions:

Discussion Question: What stands out most to you in this whole study?

Discussion Question: How has this study affected your relationship to God?

Discussion Question: What do you plan to do with the rest of your life?

This book was produced by the Christian Literature Crusade. We hope it has been helpful to you in living the Christian life. CLC is a literature mission with ministry in over 40 countries worldwide. If you would like to know more about us, or are interested in opportunities to serve with a faith mission, we invite you to write to:

Christian Literature Crusade
P.O. Box 1449
Fort Washington, PA 19034